New York

20 things to know about the credit card surcharge ordinance

Navin Vett

Table Of Contents

Introduction

The bustling streets of New York City echo with the hum of commerce, and at its center is a recent change that affects transactions throughout the state: the Credit Card Surcharge Law.

This law, which went into effect in February 2023, sought to bring transparency and justice to credit card fees, protecting consumer interests while also altering the financial landscape for businesses.

This book is your thorough guide to negotiating the complexities of this new law. Whether you're a seasoned business owner, an inquisitive consumer, or simply want to comprehend the consequences of such laws, this introduction will provide you with the necessary information.

Unveiling Key Provisions
- Our analysis covers key aspects of the regulation, including surcharge limits, transparency standards, and prohibition on cash discounts.

Both businesses and customers benefit from these insights, with businesses learning about compliance methods and signage needs, and consumers discovering their rights and how to avoid hidden expenses.

Beyond the basics:
- We dive deeper, exposing the law's intricacies and potential ambiguities, such as internet purchases, gift cards, and the impact on small businesses.

- - The various economic implications, ranging from influencing consumer behavior to affecting banks and card networks, are investigated, providing a comprehensive view.

- Legal issues and developing interpretations are examined, emphasizing the law's dynamic nature and potential future ramifications.

Join us on this adventure as we dissect the Credit Card Surcharge Law, reveal its complexity, and illuminate your route through its ramifications for all parties involved.
Dive into the pages and learn how to confidently navigate this shifting landscape.

Remember that this book is only a basic guide and does not provide legal advice. For particular questions or personalized advice, consult legal specialists or the official sources listed.

Surcharge

A surcharge is a fee, or tax applied to the cost of a good or service in addition to the originally given price. A surcharge is frequently added to an existing tax that is not included in the advertised price of the commodity or service.

Surcharges might be fixed or percentage-based. This fee may be implemented because a governing body requires additional money or to cover the costs of increasing commodity pricing.

A surcharge is an additional charge or tax that a business adds to the price of a product or service. Surcharges are typically applied to the price of goods and services at the point of sale on behalf of the government.

Surcharges enable businesses to indirectly pass expenses on to customers by announcing a charge distinct from the price of the good or service. These fees could be fixed amounts or a percentage of the purchase price.

Many businesses, including travel, telecom, and cable, will levy surcharges to cover the cost of rising pricing, such as gasoline or government regulatory fees.

How Surcharges Work

Surcharges are additional fees and/or taxes that consumers must pay when purchasing specific goods and services. Surcharges are often imposed at the end of the buying process, when the buyer pays for the goods or services.

Surcharges can be imposed at precise dollar amounts, like $4 per transaction. They may also be calculated as a percentage of the entire price, such as 5%.

The quoted price of various items and services does not include the additional premium. Instead, the computed cost is applied upon acceptance or purchase of the item and is reflected in the contract or sales and purchase agreement (SPA), or the surcharge shows as a distinct line item on your receipt.

Some surcharges are simply part of the business model. Restaurants, for example, may choose not to serve condiment packets on purpose in order to save money by not providing more resources for free.

Bank and Credit Card Surcharges

The automated teller machine (ATM) fee is well-known among consumers. This premium is typically paid by the bank or other institution that owns and runs the machine. An ATM fee is displayed as a fixed monetary amount per transaction. Most ATM providers waive fees for consumers who use the sponsoring ATM.

Some businesses have implemented surcharges to compensate for the costs involved with taking credit cards. These fees are often known as check-out fees. This additional fee could be a fixed dollar amount or a percentage of the overall cost of the goods or services purchased.

Examples Of Surcharges

Many industries, like telecommunications and cable, frequently use surcharges to offset some of the costs imposed on firms by local, state, or federal laws.

When these costs rise, businesses may increase surcharge amounts rather than the prices of the products they offer. The fee is still passed on to the consumer, but in a more indirect manner.

If rules increase the burden on a corporation by $2 per client, the company may increase its regulatory recovery fee by $2. In this method, the corporation avoids having to bear the loss or the entire amount of the government levy, which is effectively passed on to the consumer.

Surcharges include regulatory recovery fees, which cable companies add to their customers' bills. These are imposed to help offset the cost of some service fees levied by government agencies. They also charge fees for sports programming to cover the premium that the cable company pays to broadcast the events.

Other examples are fuel fees.

Emergency service rates for both landline and cellular phone services

Fees for hazardous waste disposal at the veterinarian's office.

Electronic waste disposal and handling fees

Minimum transaction fees (typically when using credit or debit cards).

Most surcharges are lawful, but some governments have taken measures to prohibit particular forms of fees. For example, Colorado legislation enacted in 2021 limited the amount of a surcharge that could be levied in certain instances.

Avoiding Surcharges

A consumer can take a number of steps to prevent surcharges, regardless of the type or situation in which they arise. Many merchants levy a premium if you pay with a credit card, especially if the transaction is modest. To avoid the surcharge, use a debit card or pay with cash.

Some costs apply due to being out of network. For example, if you use an ATM that is not linked with your bank, you may incur a cost. To avoid this, be aware of the service's restrictions and discuss your choices with your bank or other network. Always ensure that this information is returned in writing to avoid any future misinterpretation.

Surcharges are common when traveling, such as an airline premium for checked baggage, roaming surcharges for utilizing data in remote or overseas places, and resort surcharges for extra facilities.

Consider planning ahead of time, being aware of where these charges may develop, and acting accordingly by deliberately avoiding using companies with surcharges.

Finally, make sure to read the fine print and terms and conditions. Regardless of what a customer care agent tells you, you are bound by any agreements you have signed.

This agreement will clearly highlight locations where you may face additional charges, and you should use it not only as a planning tool but also as a reference for future action.

How does it work?

Surcharges are extra fees or levies applied to the cost of goods and services. Depending on the product or service, a surcharge might be a flat fee or a percentage of the cost. The merchant or service provider adds it throughout the purchase process. Surcharges are levied by businesses, governments, service providers, and professionals.

What Is the Broadcast TV Surcharge?

Television networks charge cable providers a broadcast TV premium to transport their signals over the airways. The price is negotiable between networks and cable companies and is legal under federal law. Instead of raising the price of the service, the premium is passed on to cable provider consumers monthly.

What are some examples of surcharges?
Surcharges can take the form of ATM costs, gasoline , filing fees, tips and gratuities, processing fees, convenience fees, or checkout fees.

States that allow credit card surcharges?
Credit card surcharging is a fee structure that credit card issuers use to charge customers for transaction processing. Although surcharging is not illegal in the United States, certain areas, like Connecticut, Massachusetts, and Puerto Rico, prohibit corporations from imposing these costs on their customers.

You Should Know This
Many folks pay surcharges without issues. However, not everyone understands what they are and why they are implemented. Surcharges are levies that are added to the cost of goods and services. Surcharges are either set amounts or percentages of the buying price. They can take various forms, such as service costs, handling fees, disposal fees, and processing fees.

They may be imposed by the service provider or a third party, including the government. Whether you like them or not, you can't avoid them. However, recognizing what they are may help you accept the additional cost.

December 13, 2023 Signing

Assembly Bill 2672, signed into law by New York Governor Kathy Hochul on December 13, 2023, has significant ramifications for merchants because it requires disclosure of credit card surcharges for transactions with New York customers.

With effect from February 11, 2024, (i) retailers must display the maximum price that a customer may pay when making a credit card purchase, in addition to the price that is offered when the customer uses a different payment method (like cash, check, or debit card);

(ii) any surcharge that is applied cannot exceed the amount that the company receives from its credit card processor (i.e., the surcharge may only be applied on a pass-through basis). Penalties for noncompliance might reach $500 for each infringement.

The following is stated in the "Disclosure Law" (NY General Business Law Section 518):

Any seller in a sales transaction who charges a customer a surcharge for using a credit card instead of cash, check, or another comparable method must prominently display the entire cost of using a credit card in that transaction, including the surcharge; however, the amount of the surcharge cannot be greater than what the credit card company charges the business for using the card.

Any such sales transaction's final sales price, including the surcharge, cannot be more than the transaction's stated price.1.

"Seller" is an all-purpose term. The term "seller" is able to be defined as "any person who honors credit cards or debit cards which may be used to purchase or lease property or services."

From a policy perspective, the idea behind the rule is that if a product or service's "credit card price" is disclosed right away, it will improve transparency for the buyer or consumer, who might not otherwise be aware of a surcharge until the "checkout" process. "

Credit card surcharges must now be clearly disclosed so that consumers are fully aware of them upfront and not just when they go to pay," Assembly member **Amy Paulin** stated.

The Act seeks to safeguard consumers against deceit when using credit cards and to advance justice and openness.

Companies and Consumers

Here's what it means for consumers and companies.
A new legislation mandating New York companies to prominently show the complete cost of credit card purchases, including any fees, is in full force.

As of Sunday (February 11th, 2024), companies in the Empire State must reveal any additional credit card fees before a consumer begins to check out.
Businesses can either show the complete price, including credit card fees, or offer separate pricing for card and cash payments for products.

"As more New Yorkers use credit cards and EBT [electronic benefit transfer] products to purchase goods and services, pricing transparency is critical for consumers to make informed decisions at the register," stated **Sen. Jeremy Cooney** (D-Rochester), who helped promote the measure.

"My legislation was designed to help people better understand the total cost — not just a processing fee percentage — and to be protected from surprise fees at checkout."

The bill, signed by Gov. Kathy Hochul in December, also prohibits store owners from charging consumers more in credit card fees than the firm is charged by processing companies.

Under the new rules, companies cannot simply put a notice on the entrance or at the register declaring that there is an extra 3.9% cost for credit cards.

They must explicitly state how much the additional percentage will cost the client, which means that firms cannot display a price tag that reads:
"*$10.00, + 4 percent if paying with a credit card.*"

People shop at self-service checkouts
According to the law, companies can either display the complete price, including credit card fees, or offer separate pricing for card and cash payments.

"New Yorkers should never have to deal with hidden credit card costs, and this law will ensure that individuals can trust that their purchases will not result in surprise surcharges," Hochul said in a statement, warning of the imminent changes.

."Transparency is crucial in building trust between businesses and communities and now patrons will be empowered to budget accordingly."

Note that, The law does not apply to debit cards.

Credit card surcharges

The Westchester Consumer Protection Department is attempting to answer issues for consumers and businesses about credit card fees. More consumers than ever before are paying with credit and debit cards rather than cash in stores and restaurants, and some retailers are now looking to add surcharges to bills to cover transaction costs for these plastic payments.

The NYS Court of Appeals has clarified NYS GBL 518, as follows:

Merchants can charge two distinct prices for purchases: by credit card and cash.

The extra price paid to credit card users must be marked and publicized for customers in real "dollars and cents" format

NYS law is now clear: if merchants opt to apply a credit card fee to transactions, they must explicitly warn consumers by posting the real amount plus the extra and cannot do so in a deceptive manner. Customers should not have to do arithmetic to determine if they are paying the extra.

The Westchester Consumer Protection Department enforces the statute as follows:

An additional cost for credit card purchases is permitted, but it must be explicitly stated in the advertised or labeled selling pricing of products or services, not only on the bill at the conclusion of the transaction.
Merchants must show either both prices (cash and credit) or simply the higher credit card pricing; failure to do so is a violation of the law.
If the retailer just displays the cash price and claims that the credit card price is a specific percentage more, it is a violation.

Merchants cannot attract customers by just displaying the reduced cash discount price.
Consumers should be fully informed of the whole price from the outset of the transaction, and companies should display clear and noticeable signage to notify and help customers.

The Westchester Consumer Protection Code contains two clauses that address surcharges:

According to Section 863.71(3c), it is a crime to sell or offer for sale any consumer products or services at a higher price than the price shown or promoted for them.

Scan the QR code to learn more about Westchester Consumer Protection Section

The following is against the law: "To add an additional fee to any transaction for consumer goods or services, beyond sales tax, and fail to provide adequate and reasonable notice of said fee during the transaction, including but not limited to the point of sale, price displays, signage and menus, and further, only adding said fee to bill or receipt at end of the transaction shall not be deemed adequate notice."

Finally, gas stations that provide two-tier pricing (cash and credit) must show both the higher selling credit price and the reduced cash price. Before filling up their tanks, drivers must understand their maximum cost exposure. The merchant determines whether debit sales are credit sales or cash sales.

Popular FAQ

With consumers preferring credit card payments over cash and debit, credit card surcharges have become an appealing model for legal practitioners looking to cover processing expenses at their companies.

However, credit card fee rules differ by state and need extensive investigation before applying them in your practice.

What is a Credit Card Surcharge?

When a business accepts and processes a credit card transaction, they pay a processing charge to the relevant banking institution. A credit card surcharge (or cc surcharge) is a fee levied by the retailer to cover part of the costs of payment processing.

This charge is only applicable to credit cards—not debit cards, even if a debit card is used as a credit card. Surcharges are usually calculated as percentages.

Let us look at an example

Consider a local dentist's office that mostly accepts in-person payments. If a customer asks to pay by phone, the clinic may charge a convenience fee of $1.85.

In the same office, a credit card fee may appear like this:

When a patient chooses to pay with credit, their statement will include a 2% credit card premium for the services performed. The patient is informed of the surcharge, and the price is computed from the overall cost.

Are credit card surcharges legal?
If you're wondering if it's legal to charge credit card fees, the quick answer is yes in most states.

Surcharging was mainly illegal for several decades until 2013, when a class action lawsuit allowed retailers in numerous jurisdictions to impose surcharges on their customers.

This case created a chain reaction in the following years, with other states supporting surcharging. Proponents of surcharging have contended that anti-surcharging legislation raises costs for all products and services and, in some situations, may violate the First Amendment.

Credit Card Surcharge Laws By State
The legal landscape of credit card surcharging changes, but as of December 2023, it is permitted in most states. However, there are several peculiarities to be aware of.

Some of the states listed below may have prohibitions on credit card surcharging (based on state attorney general recommendations or bar regulations), while in others, anti-surcharging legislation still exist but may not be enforced due to recent court decisions:

California
Georgia
Indiana
Iowa
Michigan
Ohio
Oklahoma
Pennsylvania
Texas
Surcharges are controlled by state laws and card brand guidelines (such as those issued by Visa and Mastercard), both of which are subject to change. Attorneys must also follow ethical guidelines and

should consult their local bar organization for the most up-to-date information.

States Where Credit Card Surcharges Are Illegal
Credit card surcharging is currently unlawful in the states and territories listed below.

Connecticut
Maine
Massachusetts
Puerto Rico

Credit Card Surcharging Rules:
Major credit card companies, such as Visa and MasterCard, establish guidelines and standards for retailers to follow when adding surcharges. While there are minor differences across brands, the essential guidelines remain consistent.

Below, we'll explain the most typical regulations that legal practitioners should follow while performing surcharges at their business.

- Notify the Credit Card Institution.

You must tell major credit card companies—in writing—of your intention to surcharge. You can write a letter to your bank account representative or complete the documentation available on the credit card's website.

- Notify your clients.

Your clients must also be informed of your plan to overcharge. This must be stated clearly, not hidden inside a lengthy contract or veiled by fine language.

You may achieve this by putting the credit card surcharge on your invoice or placing a sign in your office. If you pay online, this message should appear on your payment page automatically.
The credit card surcharge fee is ultimately passed on to the client, thus excellent communication of your procedure is critical to ensuring a seamless transaction and great client experience.

- Do not surcharge more than your processing fee.

This guideline states that you cannot utilize surcharging to generate a profit. In general, a fee cannot exceed 3% in the United States.

In Colorado, retailers may charge either a 2% premium or the actual cost of card processing. Because the real cost varies per retailer and transaction, most Colorado providers limit surcharges at 2% when enabled.

Do not implement surcharges on debit card transactions.

Surcharge fees are restricted to credit card transactions only. Even if a customer desires to conduct a signature debit transaction in which a debit card is handled as a credit transaction, you are not permitted to impose a premium.

- Prepaid cards do not incur surcharges.

- List surcharges as separate line items.

When creating an invoice and tallying transactions, you cannot add the premium to the overall cost of the service.

Each fee must be mentioned individually on your invoice and clearly identified as a surcharge.

This approach promotes openness and informs clients that they are being charged an extra cost for using a credit card. It also makes it easier for attorneys to manage and record processing costs, making the reconciliation process more efficient.

- Stay PCI compliant

While not a surcharging requirement, Payment Card Industry (PCI) compliance is a critical credit card payment rule that firms should be aware of.

Simply put, if your company accepts credit card payments, you must comply with the Payment Card Industry Data Security Standard, or PCI DSS.

The PCI DSS is a set of security standards established by the major card brands to ensure that all companies, processing, storing, and transmitting credit card information maintain a secure environment to prevent stolen or compromised information.
This is a set of security standards created by the major card brands to guarantee that all firms that take, handle, store, and send credit card information maintain a safe environment to avoid stolen or compromised information.

As a result, your company must submit an annual compliance questionnaire about how it manages credit card information.

Simplify Surcharge Implementation and Compliance with a Legal Payment Processor.
Surcharge compliance is always changing and not easy to navigate. However, it does not have to be a source of worry for your business.

Legal payment processors can assist your practice comply with the newest card brand requirements while also refuting any credit card fallacies that may occur.

Into Effect

A new legislation that takes effect on Sunday will force companies in New York to plainly display the cost of purchasing things with a credit card, including any fees, for customers before checkout.

The measure, signed by Gov. Kathy Hochul in December, also prohibits businesses from charging more for credit card fees than they are charged by processors.
Businesses have the option of displaying only the higher credit card pricing for the products or services they sell, or listing both the credit card price and the lower cash price.

The new disclosure standards will "ensure individuals can trust that their purchases will not result in surprise surcharges," Ms. Hochul.

In New Jersey, Gov. Philip D. Murphy signed a similar bill last year mandating retailers to advise customers of any credit card fees that would be levied before they checkout. It also prevented shops from charging customers more than the processing cost they paid.

A national regulation preventing shops from charging customers more for credit card purchases lapsed four decades ago. Since then, many businesses have relied on so-called convenience fees to offset the costs imposed by credit card processing corporations.

Jeremy Cooney, a state senator, said that the disclosure law "helps consumers better understand the total cost" of the items they purchase.

Businesses were already required by the state and companies such as Visa and Mastercard to display credit card surcharge amounts at store entrances and points of sale, according to Youssef Mubarez, the Yemeni American Merchants Association's director of public relations.

"They're making the merchants look like the enemies by calling it 'hidden fees' when they're not," Mr. Mubarez went on to say. "The only thing they're trying to do is save money so they can keep their business alive."
Mr. Mubarez, whose family has had a deli in Times Square for decades and who owns a point of sale and service firm, believes that restricting the surcharge amount to reflect processing expenses is a smart idea.

However, he stated that the new laws on pricing display will add to the workload of already stressed-out small-business owners. In recent weeks, Mr. Mubarez stated that he had to send his workers to assist clients in re-pricing things using a price gun capable of printing various cash and credit amounts for sales.

Furthermore, some of the state's rules — such as the fact that it is now illegal to simply place a sign at the register informing customers about the blanket surcharge applied to all products — conflict with the guidelines of credit card processing companies, he said, confusing some of the merchants with whom he works.

"They make these laws thinking of the bigger businesses and just leave the small businesses to go figure out what they have to do," he concluded

Conclusion (20 things to know)

The Law:
Effective Date: Took effect on February 11, 2023, so businesses have had time to adjust.

Aim: Increase transparency and protect consumers from hidden credit card fees.

Scope: Applies to all businesses within New York state accepting credit cards for goods or services.

Surcharge Limits:
Limits: Businesses can only charge surcharges up to the amount they are charged by credit card companies.

Transparency: Surcharge amount must be clearly displayed before checkout, either alongside the cash price or as a separate fee.

For Consumers:
No Cash Discounts: Businesses cannot offer lower cash prices to incentivize cash payments over credit cards.

Debit Cards Not Affected: The law only applies to credit card transactions, not debit cards.

Enforcement: New York State Department of Financial Services oversees enforcement, with potential penalties for violations.

For Businesses:
Compliance Options: Businesses can display the total credit card price, separate prices for cash and credit, or adjust all prices to reflect the surcharge.

Signage Requirements: Signage disclosing surcharges must be clear, conspicuous, and easily readable at the point of sale.

Recordkeeping: Businesses should maintain records of their credit card processing fees to demonstrate compliance with the surcharge limit.

Understanding the Fees:
Interchange Fees: These are the fees credit card companies charge businesses for each transaction. Surcharges cannot exceed these fees.

Network Fees and Assessments: Additional fees associated with specific credit card networks may apply and can be included in the surcharge.

Exemptions: Businesses with less than $25,000 in annual credit card transactions are exempt from the law.

Impact on Different Parties:
Small Businesses: The law might disproportionately impact small businesses with higher processing fees due to lower transaction volume.

Consumers with Limited Cash: Individuals relying primarily on credit cards might feel the impact more acutely if businesses choose to raise prices to absorb the surcharge.

Tourists and Visitors: Be aware that the law applies to all transactions within New York State, regardless of your residency.

Potential Changes: The law might be revised or challenged in the future, so staying informed about updates is crucial.

Additional Points

Impact: The law's long-term impact on businesses and consumer behavior is still being observed.

Further Resources: For more details and clarification, refer to the official New York State website or consult with legal professionals.

Scan the code for any assistance

Remember, the law was implemented to create fairness and transparency.